Original title:
The Key to Tomorrow

Copyright © 2025 Creative Arts Management OÜ
All rights reserved.

Author: Penelope Hawthorne
ISBN HARDBACK: 978-1-80586-020-4
ISBN PAPERBACK: 978-1-80586-492-9

Tides of Future Currents

Waves crash with quirky delight,
Seagulls argue, take to flight.
A crab's dance, quite the show,
Future's here? Who could know!

Sandy castles wobble and sway,
Kids in buckets plotting their play.
Some make wishes on a star,
While others just dream of candy bars!

Writing the Unwritten

With a pen that squiggles and twirls,
I draft my life in loops and swirls.
Each sentence a laugh, each comma a jest,
Writing my future? It's a quirky quest!

Page one says, 'Don't forget to snack!'
Illustrations of cats in a top hat!
Chasing pencils like I'm a fool,
The plot thickens, a whimsical school!

Light on the Path Ahead

Flashlights glow, but where to steer?
Not a clue, but hey, let's cheer!
Tripping on shoes that belong to the past,
Each step's a giggle, each laugh's a blast!

A parade of squirrels march in line,
They wear tiny hats, looking divine.
Following things that blink and beep,
Through tangled paths, we hardly weep!

Embers of Possibility

A campfire crackles, night's sparkles bright,
Roasting marshmallows, what a delight!
Each marshmallow puffs, a sweet little puff,
Dreaming of tomorrow, this never feels tough!

Sparks fly like wishes into the air,
Some land on heads, oh do beware!
But laughter erupts, spirits take flight,
The future's a joke, but it feels just right!

Possibilities Flow like Water

Ideas bubble, fizzing bright,
Like soda pop, it's pure delight.
They flow like streams, so wiggly,
In a world that's just too giggly.

Grab a bucket, scoop a dream,
Watch it wiggle, watch it gleam.
A splash of hope, a dash of fun,
Who knew tomorrow could be a pun?

Beyond the Cusp of Time

Tick-tock, the clock's a clown,
Wearing a silly, floppy gown.
It tells no tales of dull despair,
Just winks and whispers, 'Dare to dare!'

Leap through seconds, chase the hour,
Dance with minutes, feel the power.
Time's a joker, full of glee,
In its hands, we run so free!

Outlines of Tomorrow's Art

With crayons bright, let's sketch a scene,
Where ducks can sing and cows are green.
A masterpiece that makes you grin,
As we giggle, let the fun begin!

Smudged lines twist, as joy can't fail,
As cats wear hats and dogs set sail.
Each stroke a laugh, each shade a cheer,
Our painted dreams will always steer!

The Landscape of Unfolding Journeys

A path made of jellybeans and cheer,
With giggles bouncing, far and near.
Each step a hop, each turn a twist,
There's not a chance we could resist!

Silly signs in rainbow hues,
'Walk this way for happy views!'
Explorers giggling, nothing's grim,
Tomorrow's bright, let's dive right in!

Visions of Tomorrow's Canvas

Paint a picture, bright and bold,
With crayons made of dreams untold.
A dancing frog in a top hat spins,
While jellybeans grow on the trees like twins.

Flying cars zoom past pizza pies,
And fish ride bikes with googly eyes.
Lemons wear hats, all stacked in a row,
In this wacky world where silliness flows.

Beyond the Veil of Now

Peek through the curtain of silly fate,
Where squirrels debate the best slice of cake.
A walrus in a tux, full of flair,
Makes jokes with a parrot that doesn't care.

Umbrellas grow legs and dance on the street,
While pigeons waltz on nimble feet.
This is the splash of the future that gleams,
In a carnival where laughter redeems.

The Ever-Expanding Tomorrow

A bubblegum rocket shoots for the moon,
With gummy bears humming a silly tune.
Worms in top hats lead the parade,
While cloud-balloons blow shade with no trade.

A pickle plays chess with a wise old sage,
And laughter fills every page.
The sun wears shades, so cool and spry,
In a world where quirkiness can't lie.

Awakening the Untold Story

Stories wake up with a tickle and grin,
Strange plots unfold where chaos begins.
A cat in a suit reads the news of rain,
While turtles tap dance, driving all insane.

Magic muffins that make you float,
And silly squirrels learning to gloat.
Each adventure paints a laugh-filled scene,
In a tale where joy reigns supreme.

Beyond the Current Tide

A boat that's made of cereal grain,
Is sailing on the soup of rain.
The captain's hat is made of cheese,
He navigates with greatest ease.

The fish are jumping, but they sing,
They want the world to hear them bling.
A jellyfish starts dancing quick,
While playing tunes on a pogo stick.

Tomorrow's Song

In a land where cupcakes fly,
The sun wears sunglasses in the sky.
A frog croaks out a cheerful tune,
While riding on a friendly moon.

Puppies paint the walls with glee,
As dancing ants make quite the spree.
Tomorrow's here, or maybe not,
But laughter's free, so give it a shot!

Threads of Change

A snail with shoes is sewing bright,
While weaving dreams in pure delight.
His needle's made of candy cane,
Stitching joy, like sunshine rain.

The world is flipped, but who would know?
A hamster runs a gala show.
With confetti made of cheese and crackers,
The future's fun, no time for slackers!

Imprints of Light

A glowworm sings a lullaby,
While twinkling stars begin to fly.
The shadows dance, they take a bow,
With light so bright, it says, 'Wow!'

A dragon's breath sounds like a joke,
As friendly cows begin to poke.
Their laughter echoes through the night,
Creating dreams, oh what a sight!

Gateways of Possibility

In a world of brightly painted doors,
One leads to ice cream, another to chores.
A squirrel with a hat seems to be the guide,
As we skip on rainbows, with joy and pride.

Through portals of laughter, we leap and spin,
Juggling our dreams whilst wearing a grin.
The floor is lava, come join the fun,
In each wacky journey, we'll roar and run.

Echoes of the Unwritten

In the margins of paper, doodles reside,
Hitchhiking dreams in a pencil's wild ride.
Letters traipse lightly, trotting in verse,
Until they unite to create a big curse.

The ink sometimes giggles, the stories take flight,
As characters argue by day and by night.
There's mischief afoot in this semi-blank space,
Where the awry meets the funny with grace.

Tomorrow's Muse

A cat in a tuxedo conducts a sweet band,
While a dancing toaster gives jellybeans hand.
Together they create breakfast delight,
As sunny-side eggs begin to take flight.

The coffee pot whispers what fortune will tell,
In this quirky kitchen, we all go to dwell.
With pancakes singing their syrupy songs,
We embrace the chaos where laughter belongs.

Hints of Dawn

As the rooster emerges in shades of bright pink,
He struts like a model—what do you think?
Chickens in shades dance in a line,
While clouds make a racket, just sipping on brine.

The sun stretches yawns over sleepy old trees,
Chasing away shadows with whimsical glee.
In nature's great circus, we all play our part,
With giggles and grins, a flamboyant start.

Unlocking Horizons

A jester's grin, a pair of shoes,
They dance along with no set views.
Each turn a giggle, each step a cheer,
Horizon wide, there's naught to fear.

A squirrel whispers secrets, oh so sly,
While clouds above do waltz and fly.
With a twist and turn, an amusing fate,
Laughing loudly, we don't need a gate.

Tomorrow's Whisper

Tomorrow calls in a playful tone,
A rubber chicken, how it has grown!
"Let's make it silly, let's make it bright,"
With giggles and chuckles, we take to flight.

A garden gnome begins to sway,
He's got a plan, come what may.
With each small step, we skip and hop,
Tomorrow's whisper, we can't stop!

Doors Yet Unseen

Behind the door, what could it be?
A dragon? A pizza party?
With a knock, we hold our breath tight,
And open wide, it'll be a sight!

A flamingo in a tutu prances,
While butterflies do silly dances.
Inside there's laughter, all tucked away,
Doors yet unseen brighten the day!

Beyond Today's Horizon

We sail our ships made of marshmallow,
Over laughter's waves, soft and mellow.
In search of treasures filled with glee,
Beyond today's horizon, wild and free.

A pirate parrot cracks a joke,
While bouncing on a pogo, he'll stoke.
With every laugh, we set the course,
A goofy dream and a giggly force!

Tracing Steps in Tomorrow's Garden

In a garden of dreams, I plant my feet,
Sprouting ideas, oh what a treat!
I trip on a rake, it laughs at my face,
But weeds of doubt, I'll soon embrace.

Sunflowers dance, they twist and shout,
While carrots giggle, there's no doubt.
But the potatoes plot, so sly and keen,
Shh! Don't tell them where I've been!

Unveiling the Future Within

Peeking in mirrors that twist and turn,
Who's that reflection? A lesson to learn.
A rubber chicken, it gives me a wink,
Is this the future? I can't even think!

Tangled timelines, I'm lost in the fray,
Maybe tomorrow will just be today.
But there's candy clouds and whimsy galore,
If I keep tripping, I'll end up on the floor!

The Architecture of Change

Bricks of laughter, mortar of cheer,
I'm building a castle of hope right here.
But the architect's dog just chewed on my plans,
Now it's a slide with tunnels and fans!

Pillars of puns hold up my roof,
While squirrels debate if it's just goof.
My dream house now sports a trampoline,
Who knew that sketches could be so obscene?

Songs of What Lies Ahead

Humming a tune as I float on air,
Tomorrow's chorus has flair to spare.
Dancing to rhythms of wacky delight,
I might just take off, oh what a sight!

With frogs in tuxedos singing off-key,
And a duck with a trumpet who's trying to flee.
The symphony swells, with laughter so bright,
I'll dance with the future, till the morning light!

Mending the Future from the Past

I found my future in a time machine,
But it only took me to the latrine.
I asked, 'Where's my fortune and fame?'
The toilet said, 'You've got the wrong name.'

I tried to fix my history in style,
But all I got was a grin and a smile.
The timekeeper laughed, said, 'What a riot!'
I left with regrets but still felt quiet.'

A glimpse ahead showed a dance so bright,
But I tripped on my shoes, what a sight!
Collecting my hopes, I gathered them near,
Who knew future dreams came with such cheer?'

So here's to tomorrow, with laughs and some quirks,
Life's wild rollercoaster; I'll take all the jerks.
With a wink and a nod, I'm mending my fate,
Tomorrow's a joke, just you wait, just you wait!

The Carnival of Future Visions

Step right up to the fair of the year,
Where fortune tellers giggle, and none shed a tear.
I consulted a psychic dressed up like a clown,
She said, 'You're a winner, just spin around!'

The rides of tomorrow are whimsically loud,
Filled with dreams and a twist of the crowd.
I won a balloon shaped like a cat,
But it popped when I sat – oh, imagine that!

In tents filled with laughter, I searched for a clue,
Reality's funny, a slip and a boo!
The fortune read, 'You'll eat lots of pie,'
At the carnival of futures, oh my, oh my!

So grab your tickets, let's dance and let's play,
With cotton candy futures, let's not fade away.
For in every twist, and each silly cheer,
The carnival of tomorrows brings joy near and dear!

Illuminated Steps Forward

With lanterns glowing and skies full of dreams,
I stumbled upon a path bursting at the seams.
Each step forward felt like a joke,
Tripping on light as I laughed at the smoke.

The stars above winked, the moon said, 'Why not?'
I danced with shadows in a polka dot plot.
Future be bouncy, with colors ablaze,
Oh, the illuminated steps are a goofball maze!

As I hopscotch through time with a wobbly shoe,
I thought what a sight it is to be you.
The path may be silly, the journey a jest,
Yet each laugh and grin feels like the best quest.

So onward I go, with silliness bold,
Each illuminated step is a story to be told.
For future's no burden, but a laugh in disguise,
In this wacky adventure, I'll reach for the skies!

A Dance Beyond Time

In a tutu made of cheese,
We twirl beneath the trees.
The squirrels join in our prance,
A waltz of whimsy and chance.

Tick-tock goes the clock,
But we laugh and let it mock.
With every hop and skip,
We sail on a jellyfish ship.

The moon's a giant disco ball,
We throw confetti, watch it fall.
Future pranks we scribble down,
Tomorrow wears a goofy crown.

So come and join this merry spree,
In our time-bending jubilee.
With giggles as our guiding light,
We'll dance until the stars ignite.

Seeds of Tomorrow

Plant a seed in pancake mix,
Watch it grow, we'll try new tricks.
Maple syrup raining down,
Sticky cornstalks wear a crown.

Frogs in tutus jump and croak,
They spin around, what a joke!
A garden full of jellybeans,
With gummy worms in leafy screens.

We water dreams with laughter's spray,
In a garden where we play.
The flowers giggle, bloom and bend,
A blooming world, with funny trends.

So let's plant hope, and silliness,
In every bite, a bit of mess.
Tomorrow's harvest full of cheer,
With sweetness that we hold so dear.

Whispers of a New Dawn

The rooster crows in silly rhymes,
As breakfast dances, full of chimes.
A pancake flips, a syrup slide,
With jellybeans, our rolling tide.

The sunlight sneezes, shines so bright,
In pajamas, we take flight.
With toast that sings a lullaby,
We soar like pancakes in the sky.

The day begins with giggles loud,
As rainbows wear their fluffy shroud.
Each whisper tickles space and time,
In a world where silliness climbs.

So here's to mornings bright and spry,
Where laughter flutters, oh so high.
Let's greet the dawn, with joy and glee,
Tomorrow's whispers set us free.

A Doorway to Possibility

Open wide the fridge of dreams,
Where pickles dance in silly teams.
A doorway made of gumdrops bright,
Sweets and giggles fill the night.

With socks that sing and shoes that prance,
We take a step into the dance.
The walls are lined with jelly jars,
Each one holds our tallest stars.

Through the portal, laughter springs,
As cupcakes sprout their frosting wings.
A wonderland of quirky sights,
Where chaos rules and joy ignites.

So dare to leap and trip on cheer,
In a universe where fun is near.
A doorway wide, let's forge ahead,
With dreams that dance and laughter spread.

Unlocking Future Dreams

In a world of socks that don't match,
We search the fridge for a midnight snack.
Dreams fly by on roller skates,
Or tumble down like ice cream flakes.

Llamas in ties send faxes from Mars,
While cats ride bikes and throw candy bars.
Future's a circus, full of cheer,
Where we juggle wishes and sometimes beer.

Invisible penguins play hopscotch too,
With unicorns that sing a happy tune.
Mistakes are just laughs in disguise,
Future's a sitcom; we wear goofy ties.

With clocks that tick to the beat of a song,
We dance with time, it won't be long.
We find the bright side in rain clouds gray,
Silly dreams lead us on our way.

Beyond the Horizon's Edge

Sunsets painted in silly hues,
With jellybeans stuck to our shoes.
We chase the stars on pogo sticks,
Making plans with a bag of tricks.

Aliens join our game of charades,
As we dance down the intergalactic parades.
With laughter echoing off the moon,
Every night is a brand new tune.

Foggy mornings with toast in the sky,
Birds wearing hats as they pass us by.
Future adventures await to be found,
In towns where giggles are the only sound.

We surf the waves on chocolate bars,
And collect wishes from candy jars.
Every turn is a twist of surprise,
In the lands where our fun never dies.

Gates of Infinite Hope

Through gates where squirrels wear capes,
We sail in boats made of mashed grapes.
With laughter ringing through the air,
Each moment spins like a wild fair.

Jumping over puddles of lemonade,
We frolic in dreamlands never to fade.
Giraffes play poker while we all sing,
In a world bursting with zany things.

Mirrors that show our future selves,
Dancing with puppets upon big shelves.
Every giggle unlocks a door,
To a room filled with joy and more!

So let's paint rainbows on windy days,
And sprinkle sunshine in all our plays.
Hope is a joke, just waiting to land,
With every chuckle, we lend a hand.

Tomorrow's Promise in Plain Sight

Underneath the moon made of cheese,
We ride on scooters powered by bees.
Future dances like a silly old clown,
Wearing big shoes and a bright polka gown.

We keep our dreams in bubblegum jars,
And travel by train powered by stars.
Raccoons in tuxedos run the show,
As we laugh and shine with a joyful glow.

Chasing down dreams that giggle and sigh,
With dancing flowers that wave goodbye.
Tomorrow's a party, no need to hide,
With smiles so big, we burst with pride.

So let's twirl in circles until we all fall,
And paint every wall with fun for all.
In a world where the strange feels just right,
We find our tomorrow in pure delight.

Where Dreams Take Flight

In a land where socks can dance,
A two-step shuffle for every chance.
The moon wears shades, the sun trades hats,
And kittens chair the fitting chats.

With pancakes flipping in the breeze,
And ice cream flowing from the trees.
Where laughter ripples like a stream,
Life's a perpetual, wobbly dream.

Each hiccup's but a chance to fly,
To zoom like bees, and soar up high.
The clouds play tag, the stars misbehave,
In a whimsical world, we laugh and rave.

So tie your shoelaces, off we go,
To ride on whimsy, all aglow.
Skip down the lane, and twirl around,
In this jolly wonderland, joys abound.

Seeds Sprouting in the Dawn

A garden wake-up, sprouts with glee,
Tomatoes giggle, peas climb a tree.
Radishes dressed in polka dots,
While daisies wear their fancy pots.

Worms doing yoga, oh what a sight,
Bouncing beetles join in the light.
Sunshine sprinkles, a laughter spree,
Each seedling grinning, "Look at me!"

With butterflies in party hats,
Bees buzzing tunes, like furry spats.
The daisies gossip, the lilies perform,
In the warm sunlight, all off the norm.

So plant those dreams in the soil so rich,
Water with joy, and give them a pitch.
Watch them sprout with all of their might,
In this dawn's dance, everything's bright.

Sculpting a Brighter Tomorrow

With a chisel made of sunshine beams,
We carve our lives from giggling dreams.
Each laugh's a stroke, each cheer a line,
Crafting sculptures that shimmer and shine.

A donut for a nose, a cake for a hat,
This sculpture's quirky, imagine that!
With marshmallow puffs and jellybean eyes,
We fashion our future in sweet little sighs.

Glue on the giggles and paint with zest,
Every blunder's a chance to jest.
Molding moments, let's not stall,
In this funny art, we're having a ball.

So grab a friend and let's parade,
Through our playful, imaginative trade.
Together we'll sculpt, so fun and bright,
Tomorrow's masterpiece, pure delight.

A Tidal Wave of New Beginnings

Nosediving into a wave of cheer,
With surfboards made of pizza, steer.
The ocean giggles, splashes about,
As seagulls dance and scream with clout.

Riding currents made of jelly, oh!
We leap and twirl, go with the flow.
Dolphins juggle, the seaweed sways,
Cheeseburgers moonwalk, what a craze!

A tidal wave of dreams to catch,
In flip-flop style, we make our match.
The wave brings joy, it's bubbly and light,
Splashing humor both day and night.

So grab your floaties, join the fun,
Under the rays, we dance and run.
With every splash, a goofball's claim,
In this new beginning, life's a game.

Mapping the Unknown

With a map that's upside down,
I wander through my town.
Every 'X' marks a surprise,
A rubber chicken in disguise!

Uncharted lands of socks and shoes,
Where the dogs pretend to snooze.
I skip past trees with jokes to share,
Giggles float upon the air.

Bouncy roads with silly signs,
Where spaghetti grows on vines.
In this world, I laugh and play,
Tomorrow's chaos brightens my day.

So bring your hats, your silly puns,
Let's explore and have some fun!
With laughter high, we boldly roam,
Finding treasure everywhere we comb.

Glimmers of What's Next

In a world where ducks wear hats,
And squirrels gossip with the cats.
Each glimmer hints at crazy schemes,
Like running on clouds or juggling beams!

Balloons that lead to marshmallow land,
Where ice cream cones grow from the sand.
The sun winks, makes a funny face,
While giggling fairies start the race!

Tomorrow's here with whipped cream shoes,
And unicorns who share the news.
Laughing through each twist and bend,
Joy unwrapped, we'll never end!

So let's chase dreams, both big and small,
With smiles and giggles, we'll have it all.
In this kooky world, we'll gleefully soar,
Turning 'what's next' into a funny encore!

Embraces Yet to Come

Hug a tree and dance around,
With every twirl, silliness found.
Embraces creeping closer near,
Watch out for the ticklish deer!

Grinning clouds drift through the skies,
With popcorn falling from their eyes.
Expecting hugs from strangers soon,
At the big, bright, bouncy moon!

Laughter wraps around us tight,
As we leap into the night.
What awaits, we cannot see,
But I know it's filled with glee!

So gather 'round, don't miss the fun,
New adventures will soon be spun.
With every hug, the world is bright,
Embraces lead to pure delight!

Portals of the Future

Step through doors made out of cheese,
Where time tickles just as you please.
Jump into a whirlpool of socks,
Where owls in bowties play paradox!

Each portal flings us far and wide,
To worlds where chocolate rivers slide.
We bounce on clouds that taste like pie,
With silly giggles as we fly!

Tomorrow's waiting, decked in flair,
In underpants that flap in air.
With silly hats and shoes that squeak,
It's fun and games each day of the week!

So hold my hand, let's jump on through,
To portals bright and colored blue.
With laughter echoing, we delight,
The future's funny, bold, and bright!

Beyond Yesterday's Shadow

In the fridge, last week's lunch,
Whispers of a cheesy crunch.
Beneath the leftovers, hope does hide,
A mayonnaise miracle at my side.

Yesterday's troubles take a nap,
While I plot my next snack attack.
Countless dreams in a scone's glaze,
Tomorrow might just surprise us in praise.

Boredom lurks like a wary cat,
But dance, I shall, in a cozy hat.
Swinging my spoon like a wand of fate,
Oh, the mischief I shall create!

So raise your fork, let's make a toast,
To yesterday's jokes, we'll all roast!
Laughter is the ticket we must embrace,
To frolic in tomorrow's silly space.

Corners of Infinity

In a universe with waffles galore,
Cosmic syrup spills on the floor.
Aliens dance in conga lines,
Trading secrets for breakfast signs.

Time machines are old film reels,
Playing in loops, giving squeaky squeals.
Hop inside the toaster's glow,
Let's burn some bread while we go!

Chocolate rain falls from the sky,
With sprinkles swirling, oh my, oh my!
We'll surf the waves of silly dreams,
In a world where nothing is as it seems.

So grab that slice of life today,
And join the dance; don't delay!
We're cooking up tomorrow's stew,
In corners where all the laughter grew.

Futures in Bloom

In a garden where giggles sprout,
Lollipops overgrow, there's laughter about.
Sunflowers wish on a candy breeze,
Tickling the flowers with fizzy tease.

Dandelions whisper playful schemes,
To tickle the sky while we nap in dreams.
Goldfish sing in harmony bright,
As pinwheels spin in sheer delight.

Shovels made of chocolate bars,
Digging up wishes, reaching for stars.
Tomorrow's blooms wear socks with stripes,
And bubblegum laughter loops like pipes.

So join the revelry, pick a bloom,
In the garden of giggles, there's always room!
We'll plant our hopes, let them take flight,
In futures where every day is bright.

Wings of Potential

With pancakes strapped on just like wings,
I'll soar above the funny things.
Balloons tied to my silly shoes,
Let's fly around; there's nothing to lose!

I met a frog who ate a pie,
He said, 'Tomorrow, let's both fly!'
We hopped in bubbles, oh what a sight,
Chasing rainbows, feeling quite bright.

Silly hats were our guiding stars,
Navigating life with candy bars.
Each hiccup turned to a gleeful song,
As we danced and pranced all night long.

So take a leap with me today,
In a world where we laugh and play.
With wings of dreams, we'll dare to roam,
In a sky that feels just like home.

The Ascent into Daybreak

I woke up late, my hair a fright,
Chasing the sun, oh what a sight!
My coffee's gone, my toast's a brick,
But with a smile, I innovate quick.

The ladder's missing, I'll take a jog,
To climb those rays like a lazy dog.
A sippy cup filled with dreams so bright,
Who knew mornings could start with a fight?

The rooster crows, I beg him cease,
He sleeps till noon, now that's true peace!
I'll barter with him, an egg for a snooze,
Let me ascend! I can't lose!

As day begins, I bounce in place,
With mismatched socks; what's wrong with grace?
The world awaits; I've got to run,
Let's rise with laughter, it'll be fun!

Illumination of Hidden Roads

The map is upside down, oh what a treat,
My compass points south when I head to east.
With every step on gravel and grass,
I find new paths, oh boy, what a class!

The shadows dance in the bright moonlight,
A raccoon joined in, what a sight!
He steals my snacks; I chase in glee,
This road less traveled, it sure is free!

A phone GPS, I'd rather not use,
I'd miss those silly sights I peruse.
With every wrong turn, I can't complain,
New friends in the bushes, they each have a name!

So off I go, with snacks for the ride,
An umbrella, too, for the momentary slide.
Hidden roads are a puzzle and prize,
Let's giggle our way to the sunrise!

A Horizon Yet to be Drawn

With crayons in hand, I doodle the sky,
A chicken in space, oh my, oh my!
My horizon's wobbly, just like my chair,
But laughter's the color that's always fair.

The sun's a pizza, the clouds are cheese,
Drawing sunshine brings me to my knees.
A rainbow march? What a silly thought,
When every hue's at battle, oh what I've wrought!

A ruler's too straight for the curves I need,
Creating my world, it dances with speed.
I'll sketch a juggle of giggles and cheer,
With every odd line, I shed my fear.

So here I stand with my crayons aglow,
Every smear on the paper, a joyful flow.
A horizon made of whimsy and fun,
Here's to tomorrow, let's roll! Let's run!

Lanterns on the Journey Forward

I packed my lanterns, two and a half,
One's full of giggles, the other, a laugh.
Skipping through shadows, I'm never alone,
Casting light on my path with a silly tone.

A frog in a hat joins the glowing parade,
With a leap and a hop, he's not afraid.
Each lantern flickers with tales to impart,
Silly stories that warm the heart.

The road gets rocky, I start to sway,
But laughter's my guide, come what may.
With hiccuping lanterns that brighten the night,
I'll stumble and dance, all will be right.

So hold my lantern, let's make it a show,
Traveling together, through joy's flow.
Each step we take is a glow and a giggle,
For life's just a dance, with a little wiggle!

Timeless Possibilities Await

In a land where socks roam free,
And every snail holds a cup of tea,
Lemonade rains and puddles of jam,
Dance like a wild sweet little lamb.

The sun wears shades; the clouds are sly,
They trade silly hats as they float by,
A mouse in a tux at the city fair,
Juggles cheese, spins without a care.

Tomorrow giggles at yesterday's woes,
Tickling dreams in a garden of prose,
With laughter as fuel and joy as the aim,
Each moment is ripe for a silly game.

So here's a toast to the unexpected,
A world where plans are often rejected,
For in the chaos, a dance may unfold,
To paint all the stories yet to be told.

The Promise of New Beginnings

When eggs start to wobble, the chickens all cheer,
A party erupts like it's New Year's Eve here,
With confetti made out of feathers and fluff,
They salsa away, just wishing good luck.

New paths sprout from roots that never knew sun,
A cactus does cartwheels, insisting it's fun,
Pineapples laugh as they roll down the lane,
Chasing after rainbows like it's a game.

Old worries are wearing bright wigs made of cheese,
While muffins hold meetings with whimsical fees,
Discovering joy in the wildest of dreams,
The world isn't strange, it's just bursting at seams.

So buckle your seatbelt; the ride's getting steeper,
With waffles and syrup, and the dancing reaper,
Each day is a chance for a giggle-filled win,
Get ready to leap, let the fun times begin!

Between the Pages of Destiny

In a library filled with talking pets,
Where goldfish recite their greatest regrets,
A cat flips the chapters; the dog starts to bark,
They're plotting a heist to bring back the dark.

Books bounce around like they're late for a date,
Telling tall tales of pirates and fate,
A stork in a top hat delivers good news,
While turtles in bow ties are set to amuse.

As quotes come alive in the margins with flair,
And ink spills its secrets; oh, the tales they share,
Dancing on tables, chasing dreams made of ink,
For every turn of page, there's more time to think.

So let's dive between where old stories meet,
And catch the wild winds on our zany retreat,
For destiny giggles in corners untold,
Each page is a treasure worth more than gold.

A Tapestry of Dawning Fate

In a garden of forks that twist and do bends,
Where spoons debate loudly with mischievous friends,
A cake with a face starts serenading the moon,
While carrots recite Shakespeare in night's soft tune.

With sunlight unfolding like a bright silly flag,
A parade of odd socks, on a joy-filled brag,
Giraffes wear bow ties, and balloons hold hands,
While marzipan soldiers march in bands.

The dawn breaks in laughter, with pancakes in flight,
As they spiral like dancers, twisting low, twisting bright,
For in this silly realm, fate's less of a chore,
It's a puzzle that giggles and begs us for more.

So let's spin the threads of this wacky delight,
Embrace every color, share laughter at night,
Each moment is woven with whimsy and cheer,
A tapestry crafted from love, not from fear.

Paths Woven of Opportunity

In shoes too big, I trip and fall,
With laughter ringing, I stand tall.
Each stumble teaches something new,
Like dancing in a rainy shoe.

With paths that twist like a curly fry,
I'll take a shortcut, oh my, oh my!
Each turn reveals a silly sight,
Like finding socks that just won't fight.

A leap into the unknown zone,
With cotton candy and a broken bone.
Adventure's just a meme away,
Where silly dreams come out to play.

So let's embrace this wacky ride,
With laughter as our trusty guide.
For every twist and silly fall,
Leads to joy, the best chance of all.

Sunsets Lighting Up New Days

When sunsets giggle as they fade,
I chase the light while being paid.
An orange laugh spills in the sky,
Like candy floss, just floating by.

New mornings greet with a silly tune,
As roosters croon to the lazy moon.
Each dawn a joke, a playful tease,
Like socks that vanish with such ease.

With sunshine tickling my sleepy face,
I run like a cat in a frantic race.
The warmth embraces, says, 'Come and play,'
As shadows dance the night away.

For every sunset brings a cheer,
That tomorrow's here, never fear.
Let's skip into what's next to be,
With giggles echoing, wild and free.

Conversations with the Future

I asked the future, 'What's the buzz?'
It laughed and said, 'You know, just was!'
With crystal balls and tales to spin,
It winked and said, 'Let's just begin!'

'What's your dream?' I curiously ask,
It grinned and said, 'Please wear a mask!'
For futures wear costumes, oh so bright,
And dance in shadows, twirling light.

'What's on my plate?' I can't resist,
'Just mashed potatoes with a twist!'
It served it up with a silly grin,
And told me where my luck has been.

So here's the scoop on fate's great show,
It's ticklish fun, just go with the flow!
With giggles and gaffes along the way,
The future's bright, come laugh and play!

A Map to Unexplored Horizons

With a map drawn in crayon so bold,
I searched for treasures of pure gold.
Each 'X' marked a spot of pure delight,
Where gummy bears take spontaneous flight.

I followed paths lined with jellybeans,
Through forests where candy corn gleans.
With every turn, a giggle ensues,
As chocolate bunnies tie their shoes.

'What lies beyond?' I loudly yell,
The horizon responded, 'A marshmallow well!'
Where dreams are spun like taffy threads,
Adventures begin where the sweetness spreads.

So grab your map and come with me,
To discover lands where you're carefree.
For unexplored dreams await our call,
In this funny world, we'll have a ball!

Keys Hidden in the Sunrise

When dawn breaks wide, the roosters crow,
I search for gold where sunshine will grow.
A sock's a treasure, but did it steal?
Or is it lost in my breakfast meal?

A cat yawns loudly, tail in the air,
It's got a secret we're sure to share.
With every squirrel that dances and leaps,
Maybe tomorrow, we'll find what's neat!

In my coffee cup, I found a spoon,
It might unlock a sweet afternoon.
If all goes well, I'll wear my best shoes,
And dance with shadows that laugh as they lose!

So here's to giggles and plans that surprise,
As I chase sunshine with giggly eyes.
We'll visit the clouds, play tag with the breeze,
And unlock laughter in life's little keys.

An Odyssey of Tomorrow's Blossom

I planted dreams in a coffee bean,
Watered them lightly with giggles unseen.
The flowers are snickering, wiggle and sway,
They're plotting a prank for the birds on display.

With garden gnomes guarding the puns in the soil,
Who knew growing jesters would cause such a turmoil?
They rhyme with the daisies, dance with the sun,
In a festival of blossoms, let's all have some fun!

Tomorrow's blooms were a sight to behold,
With shoes made of laughter and stories retold.
If bees start to giggle, it's part of the show,
We're off on adventures where whimsy will flow!

So cherish the laughter, and plant a few jokes,
Life's far too short for the tired old folks.
Let blooms be a canvas for colors and cheer,
And dance with your dreams, as the next day draws near.

Dreams at the Edge of Night

At night's doorstep, the stars come to play,
With wishes on wings, they twist and sway.
A cloud sneezes softly, the moon looks away,
As we chase the shadows of dreams gone astray.

In pajamas of laughter, we leap into bliss,
An umbrella of dreams? Oh, that's on my list!
We bounce off the craters of laughs in the dark,
With giggles that leave behind a bright spark.

Chasing shadows, we find a few friends,
A whistling owl, till the daylight descends.
They tell us that dreams can come out for fun,
If only we wait till the race has begun!

So here's to the evenings where silly runs free,
And the echoes of laughter shout, "Come dance with me!"

With dreams on our side and a wink from the night,
We'll revel in funny till morning's first light.

The Soundtrack of Adventurous Days

A symphony starts with a clumsy old cat,
Who's singing a tune while chasing a rat.
Each note is a wobble, a hiccup, a jump,
In the chaos of rhythm, we dance and we thump.

The fridge hums a chorus of leftovers new,
While socks in the dryer are dancing in blue.
They've found a key, a zany escape,
To groove like the veggies on a plate shaped like a cape!

The sun plays guitar while clouds keep the beat,
As the trees sway along with their roots in the heat.
Join me in laughter, let's all sing along,
To the quirky, the silly, our very own song!

So grab a banana, and cut a few rugs,
Let's make mischief and shower with hugs.
These adventurous days, we'll hold them so dear,
With laughter as melody, let's all persevere!

Echoes of a Bright Future

In a world of bananas, so ripe and round,
Even clumsy monkeys can leap and bound.
Future giggles bloom, as we dance and sway,
With jellybeans leading us all the way.

Silly hats giggle, they tip and they twirl,
Where candy can dreams paint each little swirl.
Lollipop clouds float, a whimsical sight,
As we ride on this rainbow, so sweet and so bright.

We juggle our hopes like ripe, squishy pears,
While the sun insists on tickling our hairs.
Each hiccup of laughter, a spark in the air,
Reminds us that joy is a team affair.

So here's to the future, in all of its glee,
Where farts and flower crowns grow wild and free.
With giggles and rainbows, we roll and we play,
Creating a world that won't fade away.

Navigating the Uncharted

In boats made of donuts, we sail and glide,
With jellyfish presidents, full of pride.
The compass spins wildly, it points to the cake,
And we laugh at the silly maps we make.

Sharks wear sunglasses, they're cool as can be,
While we snack on marshmallows, floating the sea.
The wind whispers secrets that tickle our ears,
As we braid our adventures with giggles and cheers.

Through fog made of frosting, we giggle and shout,
With rubber duck steeds, there's no fear of doubt.
We navigate futures on bouncy balloons,
Making music with spoons, like cartoon raccoons.

So raise up your spoons for the journeys ahead,
With sprinkles and marshmallows to feast on the bread.
We'll dance with the jellyfish, laugh at the day,
Creating a map where the fun's here to stay.

The Blueprint of Renewal

With blueprints of cookies, we plan and we dream,
Measuring laughter by the bowl or the beam.
Each sprinkle a vision, each frosting a chance,
To dance through the dough, in a merry old prance.

Our plans might get sticky, like gum on a shoe,
But giggles and grins keep the good times in view.
We lay out our donuts on charts made of pie,
And slide down the rainbows that flutter on by.

With wiggles and wobbles, we color outside,
The lines of our dreams, where silliness rides.
In a whirlwind of flavors, we concoct and create,
The next great adventure we just can't await.

So let's sprinkle some laughter over all that we choose,
With sugar and spice, nothing left to lose.
In this blueprint of giggles, let chaos unfurl,
As we pave the bright path to a candy-filled world.

Shadows Give Way to Light

When shadows start doing the cha-cha slide,
And night turns to day with a playful stride.
The sun wears a tutu, it twirls all around,
While cupcakes dance merrily, lost in the sound.

With giggling shadows that leap and they play,
Making friends with the sunshine that brightens the day.
The moon winks and nods as we spin and we sway,
In a grand party where joy steals the gray.

Each silly shadow takes turns holding court,
While we juggle our dreams, like clowns at a sport.
With laughter on loan from the ticklish breeze,
We chase down the fun with the greatest of ease.

So let's dance with our shadows till stars start to gleam,
With giggles and grins, we're living the dream.
As shadows give way to the light that we seek,
We'll paint the horizon, so colorful and cheek.

A Compass for Unwritten Days

A compass spins, it makes me giggle,
I think it's lost, or just a little wriggle.
Should I go North, or is it a prank?
Maybe I should just head to the bank!

With every turn, my map's a mess,
Directions vague, I must confess.
But here's a thought, let's chase a cheese,
Forget the path, let's just do as we please!

Oh, who needs plans when laughs abound?
We'll dance on hills and trip on ground.
The sun is bright, the clouds have fled,
Let's lose the compass instead of our heads!

So here's to days that lead us astray,
With laughter loud, we'll find our way.
In chaos we find the silliest games,
And write our own wild, wacky names.

Windows to What Could Be

I peep through windows, they're all a blur,
What's next outside? A giant hamster?
I must be dreaming, or perhaps it's fate,
To find a cat that's really a mate.

Daydreams fly, like kites up high,
I'll paint the skies with pizza pie.
Will I be king, or just a clown?
I'll take the crown, then trip and drown!

Tomorrow's plans? Who really knows!
Maybe we'll end up on a game show!
Let's flip a coin, let's see the flip,
I'll take a laugh, bring snacks for the trip!

So through these panes, I'll write my tale,
It's filled with giggles and not one fail.
As windows open, what fun we'll seek,
In every laugh, a chance to peek!

Chasing the Morning Star

I'm off to chase a glowing star,
I'll take my bike, but it's a bit bizarre.
The paths are twisty, my legs are tired,
But oh the stories, I'll feel inspired!

Each pedal forward, the star will flee,
Is it running from me? Can't it see?
I trip on clouds and tumble on air,
I'll corner that star without a care!

Sunrise giggles burst through the trees,
What's this? A squirrel that's learned to tease!
"Catch me if you can," it shouts with glee,
I guess I'm chasing stars, not just me!

So onward I go on this silly quest,
With giggles and squirrels, I must confess.
A morning star, so bright and far,
Turns out my journey's the best by far!

Rebirth of a Dream

My dreams are strange, they sometimes morph,
Like jelly beans in a cannon's north.
One day I fly, next I'm a shoe,
Guess it's all part of the surreal view!

A dragon sings while riding a bike,
And everyone laughs at what's not quite right.
I'll take a leap, or maybe a skip,
And land on a cloud with a comic strip.

So here we go, let chaos bloom,
With giggles and giggles, we'll fill the room.
Each wacky idea, a step on a path,
Creating a future that's full of laugh!

In dreams we dance, we waltz and sway,
With humor and heart, we'll find our way.
So here's to tomorrow, so wild and free,
In the rebirth of dreams, just you wait and see!

Dreaming Beyond the Night Sky

Stars are just wishes on parade,
Dancing to tunes that moonlight made.
Planets spin tales of curious fates,
While aliens giggle at our debates.

Dreams are like socks, mismatched and bright,
Floating like balloons in the thick of night.
Comets race by, with tails made of cake,
Shooting for laughter, make no mistake.

Laughter echoes through the galactic lanes,
A cosmic comedy where joy reigns.
Asteroids chuckle, meteors tease,
In the universe's circus, feel the breeze.

So grab your telescope, take a grand peek,
Life's cosmic pranks are fun, not bleak.
With baggage of dreams, take flight on a star,
Tomorrow's a giggle, making us who we are.

The Prism of New Horizons

Rainbows are just prisms stuffed with cheer,
Twisting their way through the atmosphere.
Sunbeams play tag with the clouds in rows,
While giggly sunflowers chat in prose.

Every new dawn brings a quirky twist,
Coffee cups dance, can you resist?
Boiling waters noodle their way to a brew,
The morning's a circus, a laugh or two.

Horizon whispers secrets of jest,
Offering trials that make you feel blessed.
Funky cactuses wave as you stroll on by,
Painting the sky with a brush of sly.

So leap into laughter, don your best grin,
Tomorrow's the day where mischief begins.
With horizons of color, let's make a scene,
In the prism of life, let's keep it serene!

Mosaics of the Yet-to-Come

Life's a mosaic made up of glee,
Each shard a story, wild and free.
Piecing together a jigsaw's delight,
Laughter's the glue that bonds it tight.

Dreams scatter like glitter on the floor,
With every step, more to explore.
Funky shapes swirl, a carnival blend,
Every twist and turn, a new comedy trend.

Silly penguins slide into the scene,
Juggling fish, a wobbly routine.
Wishing wells whisper of fun tales spun,
As hopscotch clouds leap, we laugh and run.

So gather your bits, your laughs, your charm,
Create a mosaic that's full of warm.
In the colors of life, we'll paint and hum,
With giggles and joy, the best is yet to come!

A Symphony of Emerging Voices

Voices emerge like popcorn in heat,
Popping and laughing, they're such a treat.
In the air, giggles dance, take a bow,
Together we sing, and here's how:

Harmonies clash in a comical tune,
Silly windmills twirl under the moon.
With ukuleles strumming absurdity's beat,
We'll jam 'til the morning, sweet and neat.

Chirpy birds chirp old jokes in the trees,
While squirrels debate the best ways to tease.
Trolls under bridges join the choir, oh my,
With sounds of delight, we'll reach for the sky.

So gather around, let the laughter ignite,
In this funny symphony, hearts take flight.
With each rising note, let our spirits rejoice,
As we dance to the rhythm of emerging voice!

Futures Unfolding

In a world of splendid dreams,
I tripped over my shoelace seams.
Fortunes giggle while we chase
The mystery of our own face.

Yet every twist leads to a grin,
With jellybeans and ice cream, we begin.
We'll dance on rainbows, with socks askew,
Who knows what else we might pursue?

A squirrel offers us a map,
But it's upside down—what a snap!
We'll follow paths of whimsy's call,
And roll like marbles, free for all!

So here we are, our futures bright,
Who needs a plan? We'll wing it right!
The laughter echoes, hearts so free,
Our comedy is destiny!

The Path Ahead

Walking down this wobbly lane,
I wear a hat that's shaped like rain.
With every step, I slip and slide,
A penguin would feel dignified!

I ask a frog for directions near,
He croaks, 'Hop along, my dear!'
Though he leaps and I lose sight,
We both agree it feels just right!

The sun blinks gleefully above,
I question if it's from the love.
With donuts flying like frisbees high,
We laugh until we touch the sky.

Alas! The end is just a tease,
It leads us back to where we sneeze.
I guess this path was never straight,
But what a hoot, just contemplate!

Light Through the Lock

In a drawer where secrets dwell,
I found a sock that claimed to smell.
It whispered tales of days gone by,
And promised cake — oh my, oh my!

A key I found, rusty, quite loud,
It opened up a fortune crowd.
But instead of gold, I saw a cat,
Who stretched and yawned, just fancy that!

We danced with rays of sunlight bright,
As kittens twirled in sheer delight.
The shadows giggled, playing tricks,
As we embraced those sticky licks.

So hold on tight to laughter's spark,
For joy's the light within the dark.
In every lock, there's fun to seek,
A cat, a sock, and giggles peak!

Tomorrow's Embrace

A juggler throws his future high,
While ducks quack tunes that make you cry.
I wear a cape, it's far too bright,
But superheroes feel just right!

With bubblegum clouds and silly songs,
We skip along, where goofy belongs.
Each twist of fate is just a game,
Tomorrow's here — let's scream its name!

The forecast says, with a side of cake,
Tomorrow's bound to giggle and shake.
I'm ready for what the dawn might bring,
With a tuba tune, I start to sing.

So grab a friend and don a hat,
We've got a spark—let's grow a cat!
In all the fun, our dreams take flight,
Tomorrow's embrace feels just so right!

A Journey into the Unknown

With maps drawn by a crayon in hand,
We set off on a quest, bold and unplanned.
No GPS needed, just giggles and howls,
We'll find treasure marked by the snouts of our owls.

The compass spins wild, it thinks it's a game,
We follow a squirrel, he's got no shame.
Each twist and each turn is sprinkled with glee,
As we dance with the wind, sipping wild honey tea.

A pirate ship waits at the bottom of a slide,
We burrow on through, it's a thrilling ride.
Don't forget the snacks, or the bubbles we blew,
Adventure lies waiting, and so does the goo!

So onward we travel, with laughter our guide,
Through tunnels of laughter and rivers of pride.
Tomorrow can wait, let's just eat some pie,
And if we get lost, we'll still reach for the sky!

Pathways of the Unseen

In a world where rainbows taste like pie,
We hop on trampolines that bounce us so high.
Giant marshmallows float in the air,
And we ride them like ponies without any care.

Secret doors hide behind the fun trees,
Open one up, feel the magical breeze.
Inside, we find socks that glow in the night,
They try to play tag, oh what a sight!

We leap over puddles of strawberry soup,
Join a parade of imaginary troop.
With jellybean shields, we march on so proud,
Whispering jokes, making laughter so loud.

With each little step, the path becomes clear,
Each twist and each turn brings more joy and cheer.
Invisible threads tie us back to today,
In pathways unseen, we forever can play!

The Light Beyond Dusk

The sun makes a bow, it's quitting the game,
While fireflies dance, like sparks in a frame.
A squirrel in pajamas starts up a guitar,
Singing silly tunes beneath the bright stars.

We tiptoe through shadows of giggles and glee,
Finding lost socks where the night fairies flee.
Drapped in glow sticks, the party's begun,
As the moon hands out cupcakes, now that's how it's done!

A dance-off ensues on the soft grassy floor,
With crickets as judges, who could ask for more?
The light beyond dusk isn't scary at all,
It's a carnival magic, come one, come all!

So bring out your dreams, let them twinkle and twirl,
Dancing through nighttime, let your laughter unfurl.
As dawn plays the trumpet, we're still having fun,
For the light beyond dusk is just the right run!

Seeds of Change in the Soil of Time

In gardens of giggles, we plant seeds with care,
With sprinkles of glitter and whispers of flair.
Each little seed bursts with stories untold,
Like flowers that bloom into moments of gold.

We water our dreams with lemonade rain,
And watch them grow wild, without any pain.
A pumpkin sings opera; a cabbage can dance,
As we twirl 'round the corn, giving change a chance.

With dirt on our faces, we race the slack breeze,
Chasing the clouds on knees with great ease.
We harvest the laughter, our bounty so sweet,
Like candy-coated magic, a true tasty treat.

So join in the fun, let's dig and explore,
With seeds of our laughter, we'll laugh evermore.
For change is quite silly when given a play,
In the soil of time, let's dance and delay!

Breaching the Veil of Today

A squirrel wearing shades, oh what a sight,
Planning his heist under the moonlight.
With acorn ambitions, he sets to explore,
Nibbling on dreams, he's always wanting more.

He finds an old map, drawn in crayon blue,
Leading to treasures he hopes to accrue.
But all he discovers are walnuts and leaves,
Oh, the playful irony of what he believes!

Such is our quest, with plans that we sketch,
Chasing the laughter, our dreams we fetch.
And when we grow weary, with hiccups and cheer,
We dance in the chaos, our doubt disappears!

So here's to the days where we giggle and trot,
With squirrels in shades, grasping all that they've got.
We may not find gold, but the joy fills our cup,
In this whimsical journey, we're never stuck!

The Alchemy of Hope

A baker named Fred mixed joy with despair,
His cakes tried to fly, but they stuck to the air.
With sprinkles of laughter and frosting of glee,
He whisked up delights, as sweet as can be.

He dreamed of a cupcake that sings when you bite,
But all he created was a cake that took flight.
Off it went soaring, taking friends with it,
While he stood below, in a floury fit!

Yet Fred just chuckled, with eyes full of gleam,
For every wild flight comes from a whimsical dream.
So sprinkle your hopes like confetti on cake,
And laugh through the mishaps, for laughter's no fake!

In the rhythm of baking and sugar-glazed fate,
We find that the journey's what makes us elate.
So raise up your whisks and dance with our muse,
In the alchemy of dreams, there's nothing to lose!

Shaping Tomorrow's Landscape

A garden of giggles grew wild in the sun,
With daisies that danced and said, 'Let's have fun!'
They weren't just plants, they had playful charms,
Tickling the breeze with their soft, fuzzy arms.

The veggies were gossiping, sharing their woes,
While carrots declared it was time to compose.
'Tomorrow's our stage!' they joyfully croaked,
In this whimsical patch, where laughter awoke.

So let's plant our wishes, like seeds in the dirt,
With each silly thought, and an ounce of absurd.
As weeds may arise, we'll dance through the mess,
For in every odd moment, we thrive to impress!

In this landscape of laughter, we'll mold and we'll sway,
Finding joy in the process, come join in the play.
For the future's a canvas, just begging to bloom,
With colors of humor that chase away gloom!

Pilgrims of the Next Chapter

A flock of odd ducks set out on a quest,
With hats and canes, they looked quite the best.
They ventured through puddles, and quacked with delight,

Searching for wisdom, wherever it might.

"Oh look!" said one duck, "a shoe from the past!
Surely it holds secrets from journeys so vast!"
But it turned out to be a lost flip-flop instead,
Just floating reminders of dreams left widespread.

Their laughter echoed as they waddled along,
For each twist of fate was a quack of a song.
With hiccups and snorts, they embraced every turn,
In the book of their lives, there's more to discern!

So we join in their antics, in hats of our own,
As pilgrims of joy, headed into the unknown.
With each quacky moment, new stories arise,
For tomorrow awaits with the stars in our eyes!

www.ingramcontent.com/pod-product-compliance
Lightning Source LLC
Chambersburg PA
CBHW060127230426
43661CB00003B/360